Music Theory Practice Paper 2022 Grade 1 A
Model Answers

CW00496734

1 Rhythm   /15

1.1 (a) $\frac{4}{4}$ (3)

   (b) $\frac{2}{4}$

   (c) $\frac{3}{4}$

1.2   (5)

(a)

(b)

(c)

(d)

(e)

1.3 (a) 6   (2)

   (b) 8

1.4   (1)

3

1.5 (3)

1.6 (1)

2 Pitch /15

2.1 (a) G   (b) D   (c) B♭ (7)

(d) F♯   (e) E   (f) A

(g) C♯

2.2 (4)

2.3 (a)   (b)   (c)   (d) (4)

3 Keys and Scales /15

3.1 (1)

3.2 (1)

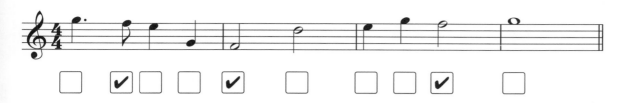

3.5 (a) **TRUE** (4)

(b) **FALSE**

(c) **FALSE**

(d) **TRUE**

4 Intervals

4.1

4.2 (a) 2nd   (b) 8th/8ve   (c) 5th

    (d) 3rd   (e) 6th

5 Tonic Triads

5.1 (a) **FALSE**

    (b) **TRUE**

    (c) **FALSE**

5.2

5.3 (a) D major

    (b) G major

    (c) C major

    (d) F major

6 Terms and Signs   /5

Allegretto means: ♩ = 88 means: ♩ ⸱ means: (5)

fairly quick   88 crotchet beats in a minute   staccato; detached

pp means: *cantabile* means:

very quiet   in a singing style

7 Music in Context   /5

7.1 TRUE   (1)

7.2 2   (1)

7.3 (a) D   (3)

    (b) bar 8

    (c) minim

Music Theory Practice Paper 2022 Grade 1 B
Model Answers

1 Rhythm   /15

1.1 (a) **2/4**   (3

  (b) **4/4**

  (c) **3/4**

1.2   (5

1.3 (a) 6   (2)

  (b) 4

1.4   (1)

1.5 (3)

1.6 (1)

2 Pitch /15

2.1 (a) G (b) E (c) A (7)

(d) F♯ (e) D (f) C♯

(g) B♭

2.2 (4)

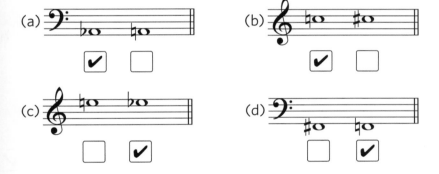

2.3 (a) (b) (c) (d) (4)

3 Keys and Scales /15

3.1 (1)

3.2 (1)

3.3 (3)

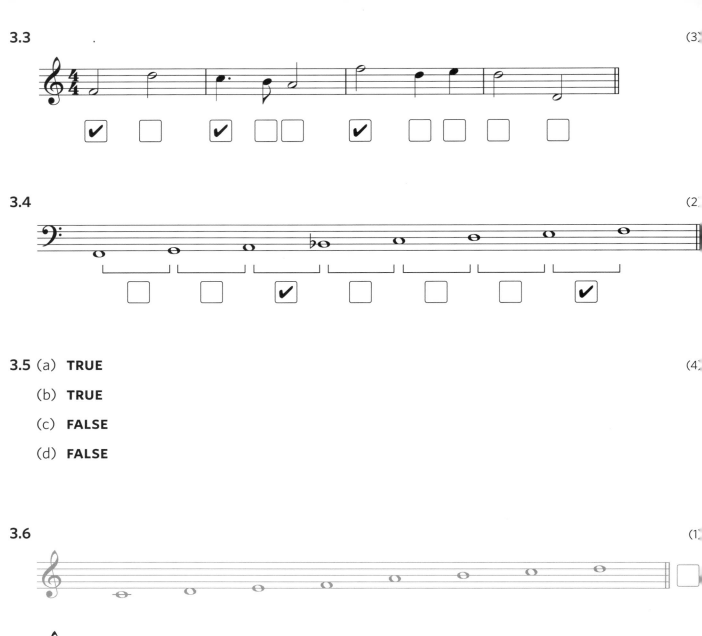

3.4 (2)

3.5 (a) **TRUE** (4)

(b) **TRUE**

(c) **FALSE**

(d) **FALSE**

3.6 (1)

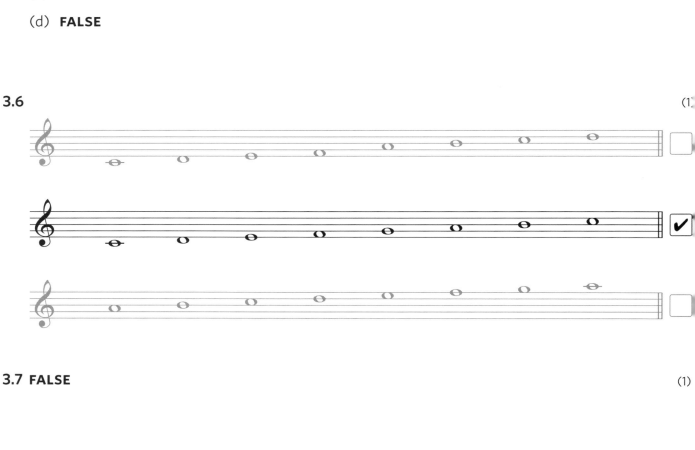

3.7 FALSE (1)

3.8 (2)

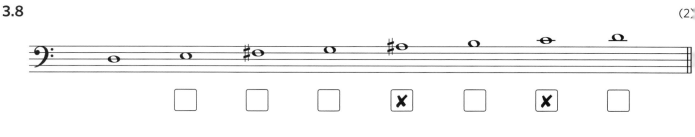

4 Intervals

/10

4.1 (5)

(a)

(b)

(c)

(d)

(e)

4.2 (a) 4th   (b) 7th   (c) 2nd   (5)

(d) 8th/8ve   (e) 6th

5 Tonic Triads

/10

5.1 (a) **TRUE** (3)

(b) **FALSE**

(c) **FALSE**

5.2 (3)

(a) 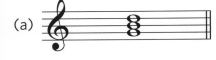   (b) 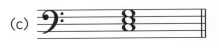   (c)

5.3 (a) C major (4)

(b) F major

(c) D major

(d) G major

6 Terms and Signs

Allegro means:

quick

means:

tie; hold for the value of both notes

mp means:

moderately quiet

(5.

dolce means:

sweet

C means:

four crotchet beats in a bar

7 Music in Context

7.1 FALSE

(1)

7.2 bar 6

(1)

7.3 (a) semiquaver

(3)

(b) bar 1

(c) F

1 Rhythm   /15

1.1 (a) **3/4**   (3)

(b) **2/4**

(c) **4/4** .

1.2   (5)

(a)

(b)

(c)

(d)

(e)

1.3 (a) 2   (2)

(b) 12

1.4   (1)

1.5 (3)

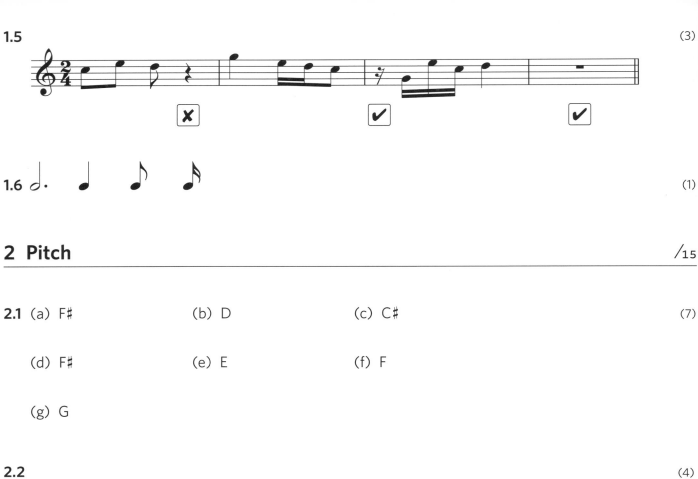

1.6 (1)

2 Pitch /15

2.1 (a) F♯   (b) D   (c) C♯   (7)

     (d) F♯   (e) E   (f) F

     (g) G

2.2 (4)

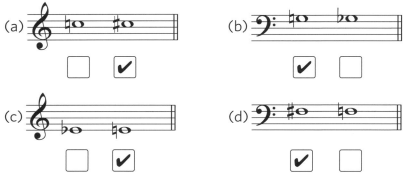

2.3 (a)   (b)   (c)   (d) (4)

3 Keys and Scales /15

3.1 (1)

3.2 (1)

3.3 (3)

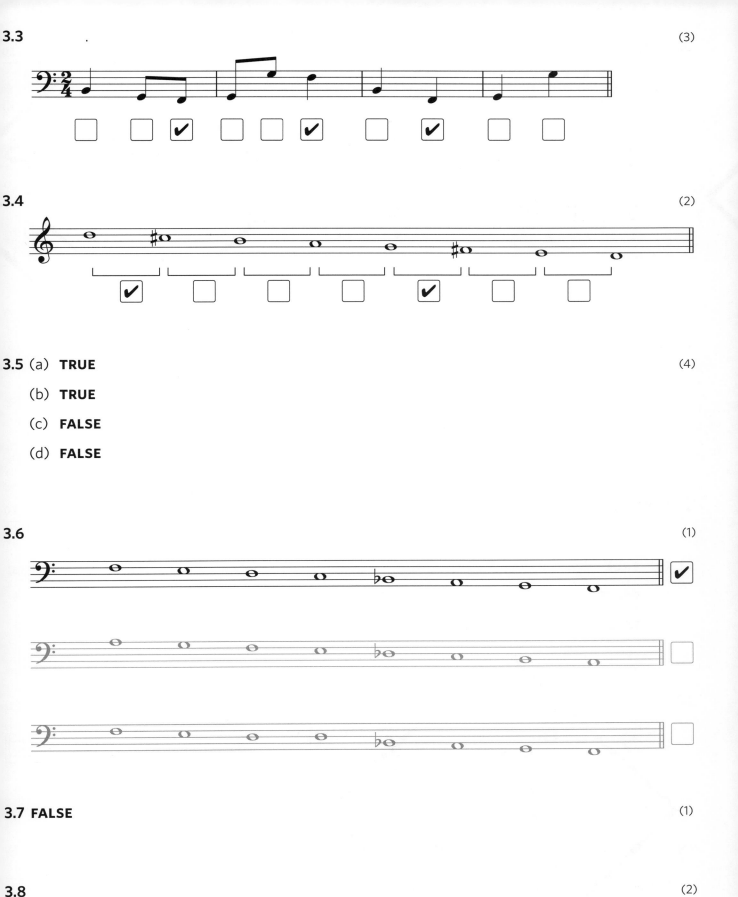

3.4 (2)

3.5 (a) **TRUE** (4)

(b) **TRUE**

(c) **FALSE**

(d) **FALSE**

3.6 (1)

3.7 FALSE (1)

3.8 (2)

4 Intervals

4.1   (5)

(a)

(b)

(c)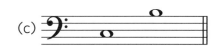

(d)

(e)

4.2 (a) 3rd   (b) 6th   (c) 5th   (5)

(d) 2nd   (e) 7th

5 Tonic Triads

5.1 (a) **TRUE**   (3)

(b) **FALSE**

(c) **FALSE**

5.2   (3)

(a)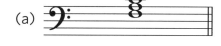

(b)

(c)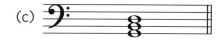

5.3 (a) D major   (4)

(b) C major

(c) G major

(d) F major

6 Terms and Signs   /5

Adagio means: *ff* means: ⌢ means: (5)

slow   very loud   pause on the note or rest

al fine means: *decrescendo* means:

up to the end   gradually getting quieter

7 Music in Context   /5

7.1 FALSE   (1)

7.2 2   (1)

7.3 (a) dotted minim   (3)

    (b) bar 2

    (c) F

Music Theory Practice Paper 2022 Grade 1 D
Model Answers

1 Rhythm   /15

1.1 (a) 𝐂   (3)

(b) **2/4**

(c) **3/4**

1.2   (5)

1.3 (a) 3   (2)

(b) 8

1.4   (1)

1.5   (3)

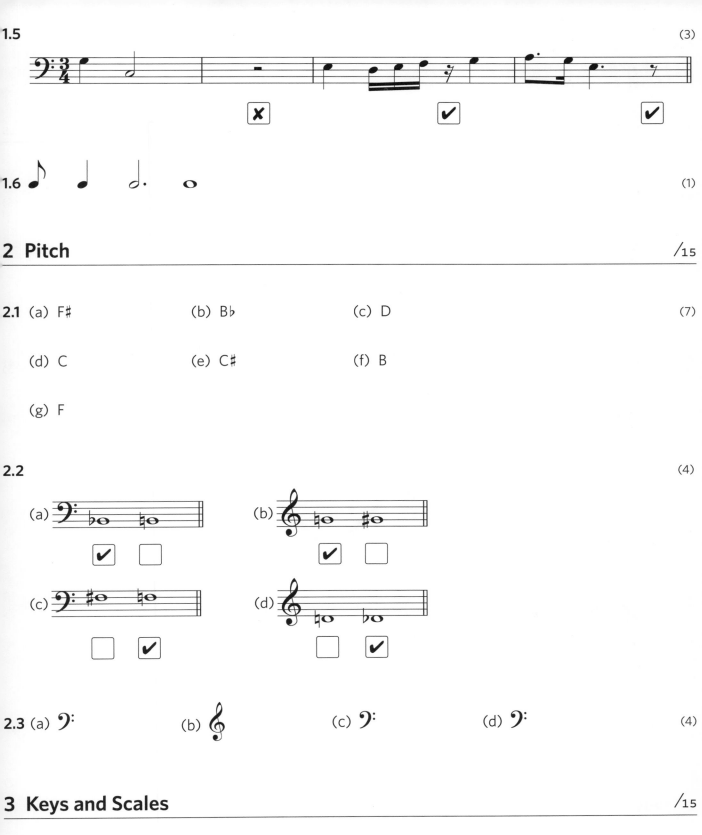

2 Pitch   /15

2.1 (a) F♯   (b) B♭   (c) D   (7)

(d) C   (e) C♯   (f) B

(g) F

2.2   (4)

2.3 (a) 𝄢   (b) 𝄞   (c) 𝄢   (d) 𝄢   (4)

3 Keys and Scales   /15

3.1   (1)

3.2   (1)

3.3 (3)

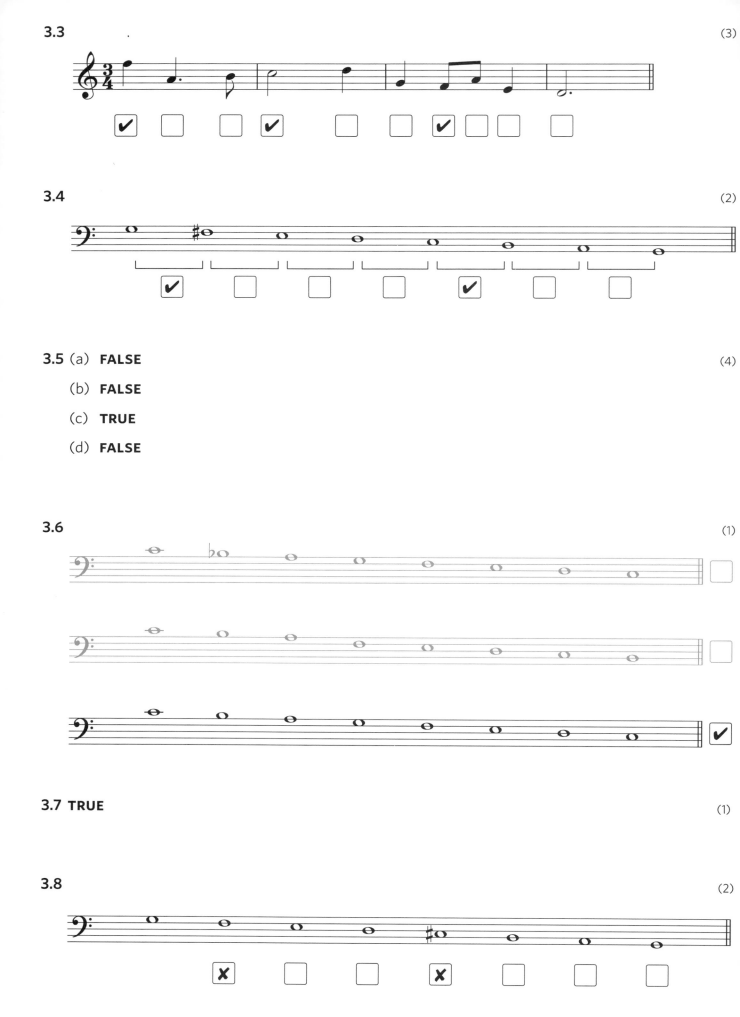

3.4 (2)

3.5 (a) **FALSE** (4)

(b) **FALSE**

(c) **TRUE**

(d) **FALSE**

3.6 (1)

3.7 TRUE (1)

3.8 (2)

4 Intervals

4.1 (5)

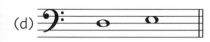

4.2 (a) 2nd   (b) 6th   (c) 7th   (5)

(d) 4th   (e) 3rd

5 Tonic Triads

5.1 (a) **FALSE** (3)

(b) **FALSE**

(c) **TRUE**

5.2 (3)

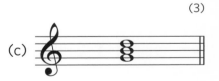

5.3 (a) C major (4)

(b) D major

(c) F major

(d) G major

6 Terms and Signs

Andante means:

at a medium speed

da capo (D.C.) means:

repeat from the beginning

mf means:

moderately loud

(5

$>$
♪ ♩ means:

accent the note

♩ = 66 means:

66 crotchet beats in a minute

7 Music in Context

7.1 TRUE

(1

7.2 bar 2

(1

7.3 (a) G

(b) bar 6

(c) quaver

(3